Published by:
HAPPY CREEK PRESS
148 High Spruce Rd.
Front Royal, VA 22630
(540) 635-2534

Copyright © 2001 by John Kovac

Layout: Weatherly Morgan
Editor: Connaught Marshner
Cover Design: Valeria Dalla Valle
Author: John Kovac

ISBN 0-9668668-1-9
Library of Congress Control Number:
2001131383

INTRODUCTION

The following hints have been collected from a lifetime of studying music. Some thoughts are original, others have been provided by fellow performers and teachers. All are designed to help you throw away your music sheets and be able to play practically any tune instinctively by ear. Whether you play an autoharp or a zither you <u>can</u> play by ear by following these time-tested techniques.

♦♦♦

The author, John Kovac, has been playing and teaching music for forty years. He has over twenty recordings to his credit. He is also a harp builder and is author of the book <u>Harpmaking Made Simple</u>. He has lectured at the Library of Congress.

The inspiration for writing this book comes from my own quest for playing music by ear. Like most musicians in the West, I was taught to play music by sight reading, probably because most of my music teachers were taught to read music, as were their teachers. I have no prejudices against being paper trained, and think that reading music should be part of any musician's training, but I also think that ear training should be equally as important. Playing by ear gives you the opportunity to think for yourself rather than simply parroting what someone else has written. Even though you don't have to read music in order to play good music, you still should understand the essentials of music and its theory. Most good instruction books devoted to a particular instrument tell you much of what you need to know about timing and music. A detailed rehashing of basic music theory is beyond the scope of this book. Even though jazz may not be the music you choose to play, much can be learned about playing by ear by reading the classic text, <u>Improvising Jazz</u>, by Jerry Coker. J. S. Bach's <u>The Well Figured Bass</u> (now out of print) can also tell you all you need to know about harmony although it is not an easy read. A very good explanation of timing can be found in <u>Solo Guitar Playing</u> by Frederick M. Noad.

What follows in this book is an effort to simplify the process of playing music by ear. You may consider this a road map to that goal as opposed to door-to-door limousine service. Ultimate success will require self-study and motivation, and you cannot expect immediate results, but you are guaranteed success if you stick with it.

The format of this book starts with a brief distillation of the essential process followed by motivational and practical hints divided into three broad categories: ear training, study techniques, and inspirational aids.

There are some general categories of instruments, musical elements, and student background which need some discussion before we begin.

Instruments can be divided into three basic classes. Which class of instrument you play will determine how you proceed. Some instruments are known for specializing in just melody (e.gg., trumpet, although it is possible to play broken chords and harmony); some instruments are known for their accompaniment (e.gg., autoharp and guitar although melody can also be played by both instruments); and some instruments can do both and what's more, do so simultaneously (e.gg., piano and guitar).

The elements of music are melody, rhythm, and chords (or harmony). Whether you are playing melody or chords you will obviously be making use of rhythm, so all musicians must become familiar with the aspects of timing. Even though your instrument may play only melody, you will become a much more complete musician if you are also familiar with harmony. And even though you use your instrument primarily to accompany (such as chording with the guitar), your overall musicianship will improve if you also become familiar with melody.

As far as student background goes, you either read music and don't play by ear, or play by ear but don't read music, or do both, or do neither. If you can't read music, you should teach yourself to do so because you can gain much knowledge about the basics of music and scales. If you already read music you are that much ahead of the game in learning to play by ear since you'll be able to teach yourself and shorten the learning curve. If you neither read music nor play by ear, I suggest you learn at least the rudiments of music notation even though you need not be an accomplished sight reader. You need at least enough knowledge to be able to read scales. A competent teacher is always an aid.

If there were only one rule of success in playing music by ear, it would be to play musical scales on your instrument until it becomes intuitive. If you can read music the task is simplified by memorizing as many scales as possible, gradually weaning yourself from the written page. You will reach a point where you will no longer just be memorizing, but rather the scales will become a part of you. Keep in mind that the ultimate goal of a musician is to have the fingers execute instantaneously what the mind imagines. If you do not read music you must either teach yourself scales or secure a competent teacher willing to teach you. The scales must be practiced *ad nauseum* playing them in 2/4, 3/4, 4/4 timing and playing quarter notes, eighth notes, triplets, and sixteenth notes.

Once you become familiar with scales, try to figure out simple tunes -- the easier the better. I suggest children's tunes and simple folk tunes. Don't be afraid to try. The more you do it, the better you become. You must realize that you can play any tune in any one of 12 keys, depending on the note with which you begin the tune. If, for example, you want to play "Twinkle, Twinkle Little Star" in the key of C major, there is one and only one note on which to begin if you wish to remain in that key. If you start the melody on any note other than the correct note, you'll be able to play the tune, but you'll be using notes other than the notes which naturally occur in the key of C major.

How, then, do we figure out on which note to begin? Melodies invariably begin on either the 1st, 3rd, or 5th notes of the scale of the key in which they lie (coincidentally the 1st, 3rd and 5th notes of a scale are the basis of our chord structures). One hint is to play the 1st, 3rd and 5th notes of the scale so you can hear a I (one) chord of the key signature. Then try your melody, first starting on the 1st note. If something doesn't sound right as you proceed, play the 1st, 3rd and 5th notes again as a chord and now try beginning the melody on the 3rd note. If again something doesn't sound right, play the 1st, 3rd and 5th notes as a chord, and now begin on the 5th note of the scale. Invariably one of the notes (1, 3 or 5) will be the correct note. If you find you are using notes other than those which occur in the diatonic scale you have chosen, then you have probably chosen the wrong starting note. The first tune may be very difficult, but if you stick with it, the process gets easier with experience. (By the way if playing "Twinkle, Twinkle Little Star" in C major, C or the 1st note of the scale is the 1st note of the tune.)

If your instrument is capable of playing chords, you must familiarize yourself with the I major chord, the II minor chord, the III minor chord, the IV major chord, the V major chord, the VI minor chord and the VII diminished chord. This should be done in all 12 keys if your instrument is capable of doing so. The chords should be played not only as a full chord with all notes sounding simultaneously, but also broken into arpeggios, as well as dividing the notes of the chord into two, three and four beats per measure. (The first beat of the measure should be devoted to the first note of the chord.)

If your instrument is capable of playing both chords and melody, then you have the further task of playing the scales you have learned to the background of the broken chords in all keys. For example, play the I chord in 2/4 time and play a perfect scale at the same time in quarter notes, eighths, triplets and sixteenths.

Timing is very easy to explain and most music primers do a good job explaining it. Executing correct timing on your instrument may not be so easy. Be prepared to do whatever is necessary to execute perfect timing while playing your instrument.

The following hints will help you on your quest. Be patient, have fun, and success will follow. ■

Charles Darwin proposed that music preceded speech in human development. Don't be intimidated by music. It's the most natural thing there is.

Like a child who learns to speak before learning to read and write, so should you consider learning to play by ear before learning to read music notation. (Imagine the absurdity of teaching a child to read and write before teaching the child to speak.)

Ever notice how you can always tell when someone is reading aloud from a prepared speech rather than speaking extemporaneously? The same can be said for music.

Practice diatonic scales.

Practice scales, both ascending and descending.

Being able to read music can take you to places musically that you may not have explored on your own. Listening to other musicians and trying to emulate them on your instrument can also lead you to the same places.

Some cultures consider it a badge of honor not to read music, but rather to teach the playing of musical instruments by ear.

Many outstanding musicians devote <u>most</u> of their study time to scales and arpeggios and only a small percentage of their time to practicing actual tunes.

Tunes are just little snippets of scales. Sometimes they go up, and sometimes they go down, and they may skip a note here and there, but they are just parts of scales.

Even if you think you have a tin ear, your ear can be developed by scale exercises.

You should be able to play scales mindlessly, while reading a book, talking to someone, or watching TV.

Try to play the scales in all 12 major and minor keys.

If your instrument has the capabilities, practice chromatic scales throughout the full range of your instrument.

I have seen hundreds of cases in which students have improved their ear and technique dramatically just by playing scales for a few months.

Try to play all tunes in all 12 keys if your instrument is capable.

There is a difference between memorizing and playing by ear. You will frequently hear people ask an ear-trained musician how it is possible to memorize all those tunes. You are not really memorizing at all, but rather playing instinctively once you have learned how the tune sounds in your mind, and once you have developed familiarity with your instrument by playing scales and chords.

Become familiar with the seven ancient Greek modes. They served music well for over 1000 years. In simplicity, it just means playing a diatonic scale going from note to note but using ONLY the notes in that diatonic scale (for example, in the key of C: cdefgabc- defgabcd- efgabcde- fgabcdef- gabcdefg- abcdefga- bcdefgab). These will sound very strange to your ear at first, but it is great ear training.

99.9% of the tunes I know begin on either the first, third or fifth notes of the scale of the key in which the tune is written.

Only about 1 person in 1000 has perfect pitch, but perfect pitch is no guarantee of success in playing music.

Almost anyone can learn to develop relative pitch.

Try singing the tune while playing it.

Learning to read music (or being paper trained) is not necessarily a bad trait.

Know your instrument.

A fellow musician once told me that the hardest part of playing a tune is the first three notes.

A fellow musician once told me that there were only about 200 tunes ever written. Most tunes can be categorized by the many similarities between them.

You can be reasonably assured (99.9% certainty) that the last note of a tune will indicate its key signature.

Try closing your eyes when playing.

Know your tune.

Tuning your instrument
perfectly is probably
the most important thing
you can learn.

To simplify timing, you can think of tunes as having either 2 or 3 beats per measure.

Remember that many tunes begin on an unemphasized beat in the middle of a measure. This is called a pickup note. Remember that if you are playing accompanying chords to such a tune, you have to wait until the strong beat begins, otherwise you'll be off beat the entire tune.

Try to sing the timing or tempo of the tune while playing it.

You may want to think of your arms as wings when playing your instrument.

When practicing keeping an even timing, let your foot control your playing. If you slow things down very slowly in this manner, eventually your foot can tap in a regular beat and your playing will keep up with your foot.

To figure out what time signature a tune is in (2/4, 3/4, or 4/4) just sing the tune noting where the actual accents fall. (TWINKle TWINKle LITle STAR = 2/4)

By stretching things a bit, it is possible (although quite boring) to accompany the whole tune by just playing the I (one) or tonic chord.

Remember that, statistically speaking, most folk tunes and easy pop tunes can be accompanied with only the I chord (tonic), IV chord (sub dominant), or V chord (dominant).

Become familiar with the I Major chord, the II minor, the III minor, the IV Major, the V Major, and the VI minor chords.

The trick to learning how to play chords by ear is to play the I (or tonic) chord and sing the first note of the tune. Continue singing the melody until something sounds wrong. Try either the IV (sub dominant) or V (dominant) until it sounds right. If you make a mistake, go back to the beginning. Otherwise you may unintentionally start singing off key to go along with the wrong chord.

Become familiar with the
circle of fifths, which is
to a musician what a hammer,
saw, and framing square are
to a carpenter.

Try reversing your left and right hands while practicing. It will first seem impossible, but if you try it consistently for about a year you'll be amazed at how easy it becomes. When you revert to playing the way you normally do, playing will seem effortless.

Make it a point to know the difference between tempered tuning and just intonation. If you can tune your instrument to just intonation you'll be remarkably pleased with the results.

Play a tune perfectly, slowly, and evenly. This gives the illusion of playing the tune rapidly. A tune played rapidly but sloppily sounds disjointed and unprofessional.

Experiment with different introductions to tunes.

Experiment with different endings to tunes.

Try simple variations of the tunes you are learning.

It's important to realize that there is no such thing as <u>the</u> definitive way to play a tune. There are many ways to accomplish a task and there can be, and frequently are, many variations to timing, melody, and chords of the same tune.

Cop-outs are very easy to develop in learning your instrument. If you can't do something on your instrument which someone else can, you may tend to rationalize that it's really not important or it's so difficult that it seems impossible. All things are possible if you keep trying. Once you achieve your goal, you can then decide to adopt or discard whatever it is that you've learned, but don't discount it before you've learned it.

The reason most people can quickly pick out the melody to "Twinkle, Twinkle…" and "Mary Had a Little Lamb" is because they know the tunes so well. When trying to pick out different tunes remember how important it is to know the tune well in your brain before attempting to play it on your instrument.

Life works in strange ways. A world-class musician told me that as a young lad he gave a performance on the zither at a family gathering. At the end of the performance his aunt came up to him and laughingly told him that it was <u>the</u> worst zither performance she had ever heard. From that moment on he decided he'd be the best zitherist in the world!

The alphabet contains 26 letters. The musical alphabet contains only 12 tones. Think, then, of learning music as being only half as difficult as learning to read and write.

Playing a musical instrument by ear is neither easy nor difficult. It requires motivation, determination, perseverance, and repetition.

Sometimes the hardest part of doing something is beginning. The longest journey begins with one step.

No matter how incredibly difficult a tune appears, you can be assured of eventually playing it smoothly and at a reasonable speed if you practice it at a slow and steady pace and always try to play it as perfectly as possible.

It's been said that Art Tatum, the virtuoso jazz pianist, developed his phenomenal technique while he was trying to emulate a favorite piano recording he owned. Only much later in life did he learn that the recording had two pianists playing together.

The ultimate goal of playing by ear should be to have your body do whatever your mind imagines, and to do so instantaneously.

Play for your friends.

Play music for people at every opportunity you get.

If you ever get nervous when performing, remember that the audience is rooting for you!

Mastering your instrument
is largely a matter of just
making up your mind
to do it.

When learning to play
an instrument, imagine that
you will play the instrument
for the rest of your life.
This will put you in an
unhurried frame of mind.

Consider playing at local restaurants for food.

Think of playing your instrument as natural therapy.

Consider recording your own CD as a long-term project. The goal will give you a huge incentive for practicing.

Each one teach one.

Purchase the best musical instrument you can afford.

Try making a simple version of your musical instrument, if possible.

A poor quality musical instrument properly tuned will sound infinitely better than the best instrument poorly tuned.

Think of playing music as spiritual and meditative.

Some musicians think of playing music as entering another dimension.

Some consider music to be the primal "stuff" of creation.

Playing music can calm the spirit.

Listen to
world-class musicians.

Have fun while playing
your instrument.

Expose yourself to
different musical styles
by viewing various musical
instructional videos.

Attend live music concerts.

Persistence pays off.

Make speed slowly.

A sure sign of a beginner is
a tendency to rush the music.

As the old joke goes,
to play music by ear, it helps
to have long ears.

Every time you practice,
play as though you were
giving a concert.

Secure a competent teacher.

Remember that you are your own best teacher. A teacher can explain and demonstrate and remind you of proper technique, but you must constantly strive to figure out why you are not achieving a particular result, and constantly seek to improve your playing skills.

Read a basic primer on the essentials of timing. Make sure that you understand timing and apply it to your daily practice of scales.

You must understand that the timing of a tune is mathematically perfect and that everything must work out just so. If it doesn't work out perfectly with the same number of beats per measure, then you've probably done something wrong somewhere in the tune. There are exceptions if the composer changes the meter during the tune, but this is rather rare, especially in simple folk tunes and children's tunes.

Learning to keep the beat while playing with others is not necessarily related to intelligence. Albert Einstein used to play his violin with a string quartet during his stay at Princeton, New Jersey. He enjoyed playing with the quartet, but the other musicians weren't so thrilled with his music skills. One of the quartet complained, after a private performance, "He can't count."

Don't presume that timing is easy. It's been my observation that students sometimes have more trouble with timing than with melody.

Sometimes play with a metronome.

Sometimes play without a metronome.

If you don't have access to your instrument, you can still practice quite effectively by performing imaginary scale patterns with just your fingers and mental concentration.

A world-renowned guitarist improved his technique dramatically while serving in the army. Even though he had no access to his guitar he invented a series of finger exercises.

Make a point of practicing every day.

Just keep playing. You'll always improve.

Ten minutes of concentrated study is worth an hour of inattentive study.

If you occasionally take a break from playing your instrument (perhaps a week or two once a year) you will find that when you resume playing, things that you were working on which seemed very difficult will now amazingly seem effortless. That is because the mind and body seem to develop while at rest.

<u>Perfect</u> practice makes perfect.

Consider playing your instrument before and after each meal. If you do this for five minutes each session, this amounts to a half hour of practice each day.

Think of practice as fun. Remember, that's why you're "playing" your instrument, not "working" it.

Your practice sessions will be much more effective if, rather than playing for a long block of time in one practice session, you break that same time period into many small time segments interspersed throughout the day.

Set aside a section of your home where your instrument and a chair are always available. This will make practice easy, rather than a chore of hunting up what is needed.

If you can't play a tune perfectly slowly, how can you expect to play it perfectly rapidly?

Once you have achieved competency, consider teaching others. You will learn more than your students.

If you really want to learn something, teach it!

Keep a written journal of your progress and shortcomings.

Sometimes play a tune or musical passage as loudly as you can.

Sometimes play a tune or musical passage as softly as you can.

Playing a tune slowly is sometimes more difficult than playing it rapidly.

Sometimes forget precision in your playing and go for artistry.

Sometimes forget precision and slowness and play as fast as you can.

Be totally relaxed when you play.

Develop some simple warm-up exercises of your own. The net effect is like running with weights on your shoes. Once you take the weights off, it feels like you're flying!

When you start picking out tunes yourself, try repetitive children's tunes. They are usually very simple tunes and they'll teach you a lot about music structure. There is a reason they've survived the test of time.

Be content to add about 10-15 minutes a year to your repertoire.

Repeat difficult passages of a tune until they become easy.

We have all experienced a difficult passage in the middle of a tune. Notice how many times we have to start from the beginning to find the passage? Try making a point of just starting from the difficult passage. It's great discipline.

Try to find some books or magazine articles about the history of your musical instrument.

Consider purchasing the <u>Oxford Companion to Music</u>, and try reading yourself to sleep with it each night. You will gain a musical education very rapidly.

Consider subscribing to a magazine devoted to your instrument.

Consider playing duets with a fellow musician. You will find that the whole is greater than the sum of the parts.

Schedule a performance of your music well in advance. A performance is a great incentive to practice.

If you are giving a musical presentation be aware that stage jitters tend to make you play faster. Be aware of this and try to moderate your speed.

Try to tap your foot while playing, or sway your head or body, but don't let this be a distraction to the public when performing.

A trick to increasing speed is to set your metronome to a challenging speed (for example 140) and try playing the tune as best you can. Then back off to a slower speed (say 120). Next attempt 140. Then try 124. Back to 140. Then try 128. Keep this up until 140 is easy.

Modern programmable drum and bass machines are a big step above metronomes.

When musicians critique other musicians, they invariably consider tone high on the list. Always strive for the best possible tone.

Learn to control your instrument. Otherwise it will control you.

Maintain a list of your repertoire and tape it to your instrument. Make a point of playing these tunes on a rotating basis so that you are playing each tune a few times a week.

Sometimes looking in a mirror while you're practicing can solve major technique deficiencies.

Try taping yourself on a home recording system. You'll quickly discover your weak points.

Videotape yourself while playing. You'll quickly discover weaknesses in your technique, as well as ways to improve your stage presence.

It usually takes only a few days to correct a bad habit once you take the big step of making up your mind to do it correctly.

Some musicians feel that playing a musical instrument well is largely a matter of correcting bad habits.

When performing don't play too long. Remember that less is more. Always leave the audience asking for more.

Try composing a simple but original tune.

Consider attending workshops at musical festivals for your particular instrument. You will leave the workshops feeling newly energized.

Volunteer to play music for the residents of a local nursing home. They'll love it and it's a great way to practice performing for others.

Play music with others.

Try jamming along with your favorite recordings.

When playing a tune remember to vary the volume (sometimes soft and sometimes loud); otherwise your playing will sound boring to others.

Listen to lots of different kinds of music.

Try to have a basic understanding of the musical structure of your particular instrument.

You should strive to play in time and evenly, but sometimes *rubato* (elasticity in tempo and rhythm) is effective.

If you have an instrument which must be tuned, consider purchasing a battery-powered quartz chromatic tuner.

To play music by ear,
just play music by ear.

Quit your day job.

I hope the hints in this book prove helpful to you. If you would like to share any hints which have helped you in your musical development please send them to the author.

John Kovac
148 High Spruce Rd.
Front Royal, VA 22630